Lily's L▯▯k

and

Ghost Ride!

'Lily's Luck' and 'Ghost Ride!'
An original concept by Katie Dale
© Katie Dale 2023

Illustrated by Claudio Cerri

Published by MAVERICK ARTS PUBLISHING LTD
Studio 11, City Business Centre, 6 Brighton Road,
Horsham, West Sussex, RH13 5BB
© Maverick Arts Publishing Limited August 2023
+44 (0)1403 256941

A CIP catalogue record for this book is available at the British Library.

ISBN 978-1-84886-981-3

www.maverickbooks.co.uk

This book is rated as: Red Band (Guided Reading)
It follows the requirements for Phase 2/3 phonics.
Most words are decodable, and any non-decodable words are familiar,
supported by the context and/or represented in the artwork.

Lily's Luck
and
Ghost Ride!

By Katie Dale

Illustrated by
Claudio Cerri

The Letter L

Trace the lower and upper case letter with a finger. Sound out the letter.

Down

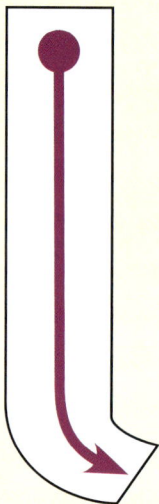

Down, cross

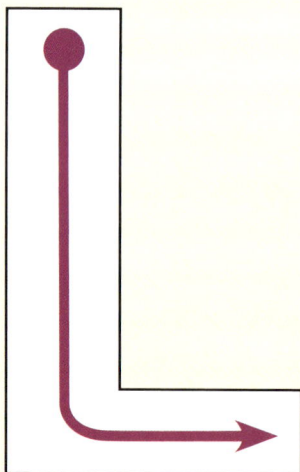

Some words to familiarise:

rocket  Lily  doll

High-frequency words:

all   the   to   a   go   you

an   it   in   was   I   of

Tips for Reading 'Lily's Luck'

- *Practise the words listed above before reading the story.*

- *If the reader struggles with any of the other words, ask them to look for sounds they know in the word. Encourage them to sound out the words and help them read the words if necessary.*

- *After reading the story, ask the reader what Lily had to do to win Big Ted.*

Fun Activity

Draw a doll!

Lily's Luck

Hit all the cans to win a rocket.

Go Lily!

CRASH!

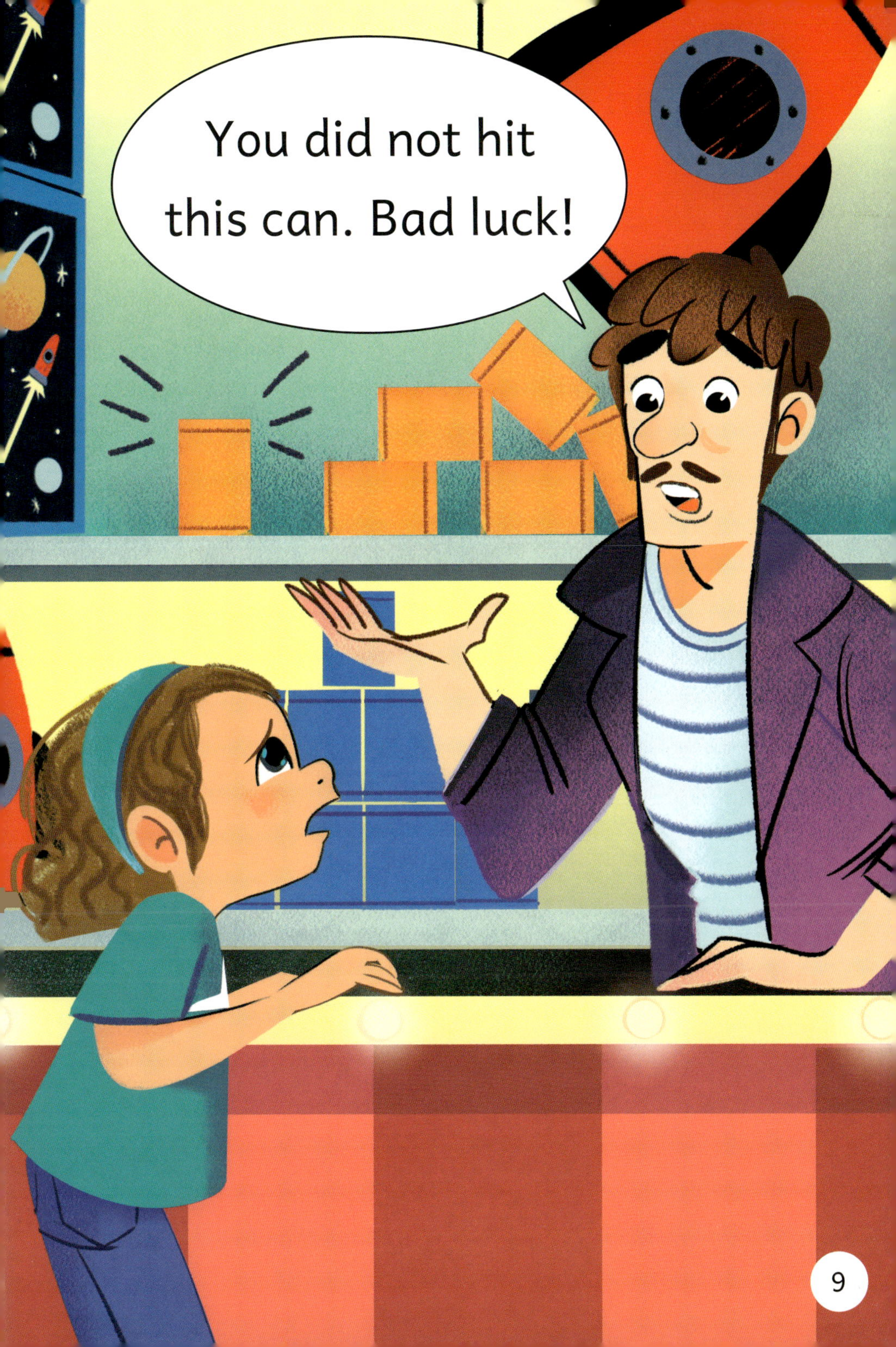
You did not hit this can. Bad luck!

Pick an odd duck to win a doll.

Go Lily!

5

11

3

7

Kick it in the net to win Big Ted.

Go Lily!

BASH!

That was bad luck, Lily!

...but a LOT of fun!

The Letter O

Trace the lower and upper case letter with a finger. Sound out the letter.

Around

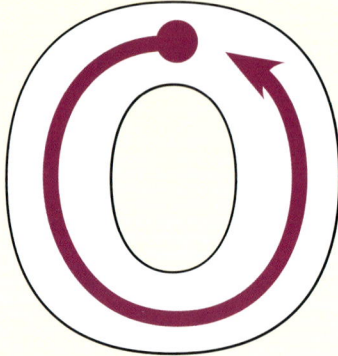

Around

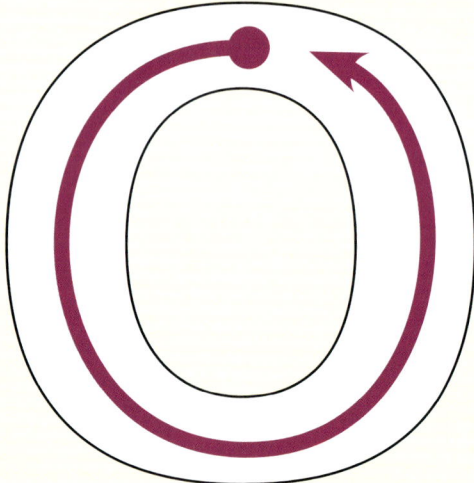

Some words to familiarise:

tunnel  cobweb  ghost

High-frequency words:

we	go	on	the	said
me	if	you	to	off
into	a	up	no	was

Tips for Reading 'Ghost Ride!'

- Practise the words listed above before reading the story.

- If the reader struggles with any of the other words, ask them to look for sounds they know in the word. Encourage them to sound out the words and help them read the words if necessary.

- After reading the story, ask the reader why Dad got a shock.

Fun Activity

Dress up as a ghost!

Ghost Ride!

"Can we go on the ghost ride?" said Lily.

"Yes," said Dad. "But tell me
if you wish to get off."

The ride went into a tunnel.

Lily got a shock!

Help! A bat!

23

The ride went into a pit.

Lily got a shock!

The ride went up a hill.

Help! A ghost!

Lily got a shock!

The ride ended.

"Let's go!" said Dad.

"No!" said Lily. "Can we get back on? That was fun!"

Dad got a shock!

Book Bands for Guided Reading

Pink

Red

Yellow

Blue

Green

Orange

Turquoise

Purple

Gold

White

The Institute of Education book banding system is a scale of colours that reflects the various levels of reading difficulty. The bands are assigned by taking into account the content, the language style, the layout and phonics. Word, phrase and sentence level work is also taken into consideration.

Maverick Early Readers are a bright, attractive range of books covering the pink to white bands. All of these books have been book banded for guided reading to the industry standard and edited by a leading educational consultant.

Cool Duck and Lots of Hats

Catch It, Jess! and Cat Nap

The Space Race

Pirates Don't Drive Diggers

A Right Royal Mess

To view the whole Maverick Readers scheme, visit our website at www.maverickearlyreaders.com

Or scan the QR code above to view our scheme instantly!